From Tragedy to Triumph

Table of Contents

Introduction..[2](#)

The Persistent Cook: A Man on a Mission to Return Offshore................[4](#)

The Tankerman's Tale..........................[8](#)

Confessions from a Boat Captain.....[10](#)

The Journey Home: Recovery and Remembrance.......................................[13](#)

A Blind Man's Million Dollar Story...[16](#)

One Roughneck's Surprise................[18](#)

A Life-long Struggle Made a Little Easier...[20](#)

A Captain Left with One Choice......[22](#)

www.JonesActLaw.com

Introduction

Our maritime law firm has had the honor of representing maritime workers from all walks of life including from more than 30 states, as well as, Canada (see blue states on Client Map). These individuals each had their own unique experiences and problems after their injuries offshore. Despite their differences, our clients share many common concerns:

- How will I work?
- Will I be able to go back offshore?
- Will my injuries put me on the blacklist?
- How will I provide for my family?
- How will I pay for my bills?
- Will this injury cost me my career?

The following success stories come directly from our clients. In their own words, they retell their experiences after their offshore injury. Discover how these individuals overcame the challenges that beset them and how they were able to move on with their lives and their futures.

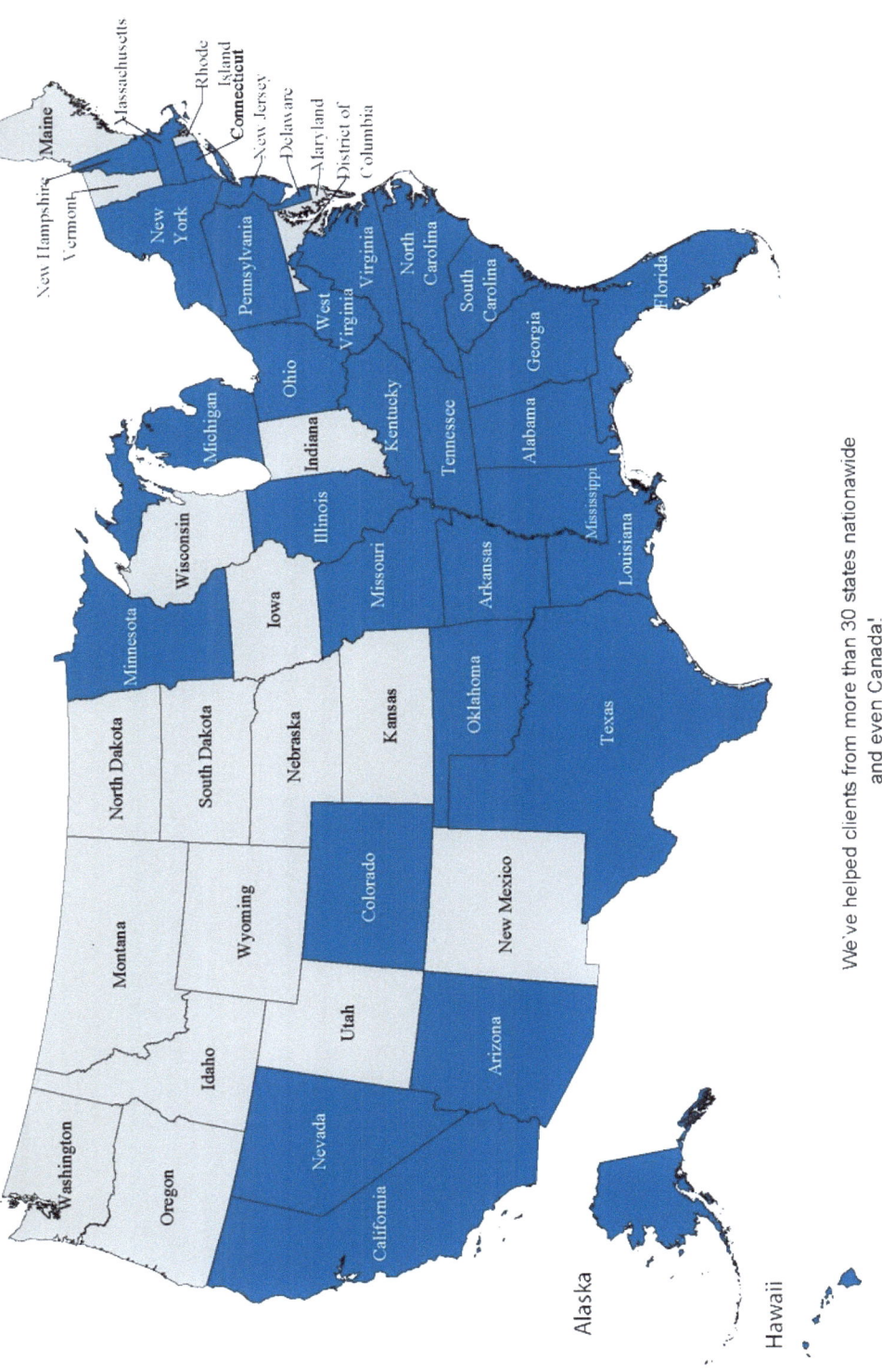

We've helped clients from more than 30 states nationawide and even Canada!

The Persistent Cook: A Man on a Mission to Return Offshore

"In the beginning I did fear about certain companies not wanting to hire me because of my back injury. But I just kept the faith and I just believed that one day I would be back out there doing what I love to do. And here I am: I'm back almost a year now to work."

My name is Joshua Johnson and I'm an offshore worker. I live in Pineville, Louisiana. I have a 19-year-old daughter who is in college at LSU, a 10-year-old about to be 11, and I have a newborn son; he's 6 weeks old. I started working offshore in June of 2005. My accident was January 19, 2009, and I went back to work in February of 2012.

I was in bed sleeping about two, three in the morning and the boat actually ran into a platform and knocked me off the bed; I suffered from back and neck injuries.

When I came into the office, I was looking to find some good medical health, and get the compensation I knew that was coming. But my main goal was to be seen by good doctors so I could get back to the life that I had before the injury.

I was looking for help and I knew I needed a very good firm to see me through the ordeal that I was going through.

After the initial visit that I had with The Young Firm, with Timothy Young, I felt better. I felt more at ease and I just felt in my heart that I had picked the right company to represent me. They really helped me out through my time of not being able to work.

He set me up pretty good with a specialist for my injury. I had Dr. Cobb. His office was down in Lafayette, Louisiana. He explained to me the options that I had with having the surgery or not having the surgery and how long it would take for my body to heal. He explained to me the results of the MRI that I had. He painted a picture of how my future would be with or without the surgery.

The medication that I received and the rehabilitation put me back on track where I could live a normal life again. It took me three years before I got back to doing what I was doing.

In the beginning, I did fear about certain companies not wanting to hire me because of my back injury. But I just kept the faith and I just believed that one day I would be back out there doing what I love to do. And here I am: I'm back almost a year now to work.

It really depends on the severity of the injury whether you will be able to go back to work. And then it's up to the individual, too. They need a mindset that they want to go back to work, or they need to go back to work. If they do what their doctors have told them to do, they can make a full recovery like I did.

I did very good on my case. It came out just as Tim framed it. He mapped it out and he gave me a diagram of what to expect and the amount of monies and things like that. And it came out 100 percent the way he framed it.

I didn't have to go to court and that was a good thing that I didn't have to fight it out. But all-in-all I had a very good experience with The Young Firm and I would highly recommend them to any of my coworkers and anybody that I meet.

They were honest with me; they were up front. They're very professional and they're patient. And they really have your best interests at heart; they see you through your pain and your suffering.

Anytime I called them, or needed anything, they were right there. I wasn't denied anything. And they helped me a lot.

I would recommend The Young Firm to anyone who is looking for legal counsel. The Young Firm is an excellent company and they really have your best interests at heart.

The Tankerman's Tale

"I didn't know how I'd be able to pay my bills. My bills were over two thousand dollars a month."

My name is Dimas Escobar. I was working for 20 years as a tankerman. One day I got hurt on the job. I was hurt in my back, in my arm, and my hands were broken. Every month I had to go to the doctors that The Young Firm set up for me.

My company pulled me off and they told me to wait to get well and then come back. I didn't know how I'd be able to pay my bills. My bills were over two thousand dollars a month. Of course, I had to call Mr. Tim. He told me they could take care of me, and he did take care of me. As a matter fact, I had another problem with the same company and they were not going to pay me. And I called Tim and he immediately sent a letter to the company. He got me my money that was taken away from me.

The staff treated me pretty good in the office. Every time I came to the office they asked about me and all the people were real nice people.

So, I recommend him all the time to everybody, because Tim is the best guy I've met.

Confessions from a Boat Captain

"I never thought that I would be injured in the workplace. I was always saying it happens to other people or other people's boats."

My name's Jimmy. I'm 44 years old. I've been working as a boat captain since the age of 18 years old, and have been doing it for a little over twenty years. So, needless to say, I've been quite a few places in the work industry, offshore and onshore; I worked on both sides of the business. I was pretty safety-orientated considering the most part; we pretty much always had one of the safest vessels that I was tied up to.

I never thought that I would be injured in the workplace. I was always saying it happens to other people or other people's boats. But I was put in a situation one day with one of my crew members, the deckhand. He pretty much put himself in a unsafe act. I tried to get him out of the situation and winded up hurting myself in the process.

I ended up going to the doctors and all and they were telling me was false instances of my injuries. I knew something more was wrong because I could feel it; I never felt this kind of pain and stuff before in my life, in my back and in my neck, pretty much my whole spinal area. So, I winded up going and getting a second opinion. The second opinion pretty much told me right away that I needed surgery on my neck. I had more problems than what the company doctors were saying. When I went back for a second appointment with my second opinion, the company's representative was at the doctor's office. How they found out that I had an appointment there, I don't really know.

I felt like I was being put in a pickle. I winded up coming to The Young Firm and I met Tim. Tim told me pretty much the scenario of what was going on. I had to take a step back and realize this. I've been with this company for over 12 years. I never thought I would be put in a situation like this. And all I wanted to do was get myself better so I can get back to work.

I have two artificial discs in my neck, and I have pretty good function. I have two fusions in my lower back. I also have some kind of messed up discs in my mid-back that's too risky for them to be messed with so my own choice is to leave well enough alone. I can deal with it. I can manage with it. So, in my situation

I feel pretty good. But if I have the opportunity to go back to work with a little bit more time of recovery, I think that I'm capable of doing it. Overall with my surgeries, I feel like I'm fixed up pretty good.

I didn't really know how this would all come to end. I just knew that there was a lot of stuff involved in it, and I thought it was going be drawn out. We came to an agreement on the settlement in probably less than a week, though, and it wasn't any hassle on my part; it probably was on Mr. Tim's. Thank God, that's what he's there for. All I did was pretty much just sat back and waited for my settlement to come in.

I didn't want to ever be in a lawyer's office. And I never thought that I would have to ever go to a lawyer's office. Only in maybe an instance with somebody else.

I did come and see Mr. Tim and I'll tell you what, he's a great guy and helped me out all the way through this thing. Even after it's all said and done, he's still there and he's like a new member to the family. He helped me out a lot and I could move forward with my life from here because of Tim. I appreciate everything they did for me. And I really mean that.

The Journey Home: Recovery and Remembrance

"I got the surgery and this was very painful. I'm not one to care for pain at all. So, it was pretty horrifying for me."

My name is Gwenn Brown from Baton Rouge, Louisiana. I am married and have son and a wife. I worked chemical plants 28 years before going offshore to work as a cook.

I sustained my injury when I fell out of a top bunk offshore. Instead of being in the little bunk, I had to go to the top because there wasn't one below available at the time.

I was coming home from the accident which is about a three-hour drive to Baton Rouge. My knee swelled up pretty much as big as my head and I knew something was wrong. So, I went to the hospital and they told me I had to come in the next day because I probably had to see an orthopedic.

So, I went in the next day and saw a doctor and that's when they did the X-Rays and determined that I had torn my meniscus in my knee. And from there they set up surgery for me the next week, the next two days, matter of fact. I got the surgery and this was

very painful. I'm not one to care for pain at all. So, it was pretty horrifying for me. They kept me on medication to ease the pain but I didn't like the medication so I stopped taking it.

From there I just contacted my attorney, Mr. Young's firm and they handled the case from there. Once I hired The Young Firm, I was treated very well. I didn't have to do anything. They kept in contact with me day-to-day, kept me updated on the progress of the case as it went along.

The settlement didn't take long. He kept me updated on the pace of it and how long it'd probably take. And I had to go to doctors in New Orleans and Baton Rouge and everywhere else. But so far as the pace of it, I was okay with it and everything turned out much better than I thought it would.

The Young Firm is a very professional firm, from Mr. Robert on down to the secretaries; they're very nice and courteous. I never had a problem with any of them.

I just like to thank The Young Firm for everything they've done for me because the final settlement was much more than what I thought it would be.

From Tragedy to Triumph

A Blind Man's Million Dollar Story

"The company that I was working for just kind of left me out. They tried to blow it off as it was my fault."

When I came in to see Tim Young, I had gotten injured offshore. I had some hydraulic hoses blow loose and blew hydraulic fluid in my face, burnt my eyes. I lost vision in my right eye.

He made sure that I had all the attention from the doctors that I needed. We went through doctor after doctor to make sure that there was absolutely nothing I could do or if there was any hope to get my vision back. Of course, there was not.

The company that I was working for just kind of left me out. They tried to blow it off as it was my fault, but that was when Tim Young came in and he tells me, "you let me handle this and we will get these other attorneys off your back and we will take care of what you need" and he did.

When we went to trial, I saw him in action. You had to see this guy in court. The jury found in my favor. They awarded me 1.1 million dollars.

He is going to give you the God's honest truth about it. He is not going to jerk you around on anything.

He won that case for me. I just cannot say enough good things about them. They are good.

You would really have to meet him in person and come see and talk to these people to really get an idea of how they are.

One Roughneck's Surprise

"He began to tell me that everything was going to be fine, just tell him what happened and, if I need anything, call him and he was there."

My name is Phillippi and back in October 2003, we were on a drilling rig and I was on the drill floor, roughnecking, and the driller told us to pick up a very big tong (which requires really three to four people to pick up) and we began to pick it up.

I could not handle my end and I dropped it, and after I dropped it, I began to feel some pain hit me in my back. My lower back began to hurt and later on it went down my right leg, and I began to wonder what happened to me. I thought maybe I pulled a muscle or something.

I went to the doctor and the doctor said that I had a herniated disc at L4 and L5 and nerve damage going down my right leg. Next, he told me that I have to find another profession because if I go back out there, I will be paralyzed lifting anything.

He referred me to The Young Firm in New Orleans and I called and talked with Bob Young. Bob Young answered me and they told him about my story and everything and right away, it was not even two days, Bob Young was there in Harrisburg, Mississippi at my house. He began to tell me that everything was going to be fine, just tell him what happened and, if I need anything, call him and he was there.

I had never seen an attorney come to the rescue like that. He drove all the way to Harrisburg and that is at least a two-hour drive.

The settlement was $250,000 and amazing. They received my money in less than a year.

He is great, even the secretaries; all of them. They treated me with love. This experience overall was great. You can expect no better attorneys, and secretaries, and even today as I come here, they all remember me and treat me with kindness and love. I'll tell anyone to go to The Young Firm. The Young Firm is great.

A Life-long Struggle Made a Little Easier

"We had 1.2 million dollars and, of course, it was reduced, but it was still favorable result for what happened to me. I still had this life-long injury that I had to deal with."

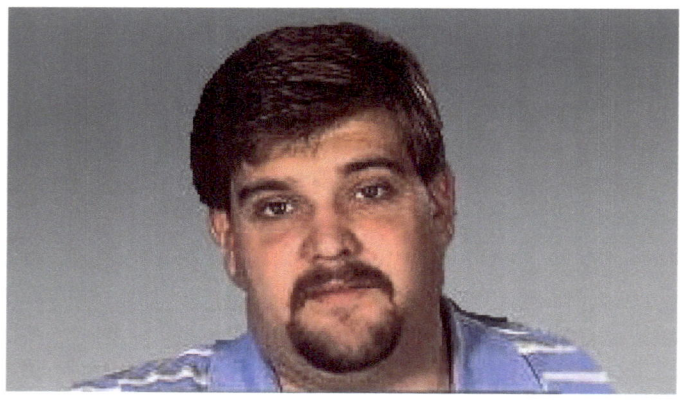

My name is Charles and I was working offshore and had been there for a couple of months. I was asked to move a certain piece of equipment across in unsafe working conditions. I was instructed to do so and when that happened, the tanks fell on my foot, crushing it and this caused my injury.

When I came in to Tim, he got me set up so I could receive the proper medical care because the company doctors that I was going to would not treat me properly and they just misdiagnosed me mainly for the company's benefit.

Tim revealed certain laws to me that gave me the right to choose my own doctor and get my own medical attention closer to home so I could manage.

The trial was very long and excruciating. It took about a year and a half before we could actually get to trial. Working with Tim was great because he was there; he was a support.

He was also on my side and he helped me through the whole situation. I am very glad that Tim was there to guide me along the way, because I would not be able to do so by myself.

We had favorable results from the trial. We did win. We had 1.2 million dollars and, of course, it was reduced, but it was still a favorable result for what happened to me. I still had this life-long injury that I had to deal with.

Tim Young is a great guy. He is very understanding. He meets the needs of his clients with the utmost professionalism. I could not think of anybody else better that I had ever worked work with.

A Captain Left with One Choice

"I didn't really want to sue. All I wanted was my hospitalization paid and everything. And they wouldn't even budge on anything, so I didn't have any choice but to hire an attorney."

My name is Collins Conner. I've been working on boats all my life, since I was 18. I've run riverboats and offshore boats, and that's 42 years I've been on the water.

Well, me and my tankerman were on the barge pulling a fuel hose up. Everything was going good, but the dockman pulled the hose the opposite way we were pulling and it caused my injury. I had to get an operation on my back. I had a ruptured disc and two bulging discs, and when I called my company to try to get them to pay the hospital, they wouldn't do it.

The doctors removed my L5 and S1. I'm still having problems with the nerves in my back so now I get a shot every four months and I'm taking a medicine which is helping me. I had a little delay on the shots because a blood clot went through my lung; so I can't get the shots right now.

I didn't really want to sue. All I wanted was my hospitalization paid and everything. And they wouldn't even budge on anything, so I didn't have any choice but to hire an attorney. That's when I saw The Young Firm and I called. They were the only attorneys I needed to call.

I saw The Young Firm in an advertisement in the phone book and I saw an honest face that I knew I could trust.

The thing about it is, you've gotta to choose someone who's going to get you what you can get to support you the rest of your life because of your family. And if you know you're injured or if you're hurting and you know you can't work, I would recommend The Young Firm because they'll get you want you need. And even though you can't go back to work, at least you've got something to help you out through the years.

The Young Firm prepared me for everything. When it came down to the settlements, I was very happy they didn't just settle for anything. They just stuck it out and did what was best for me.

The Young Firm impressed me because they all are very professional people. They all go out of their way to help their clients. That's the main thing in an attorney. The Young Firm did everything I wanted done plus more. I was very impressed.

I have already recommended two people to call. But I would recommend The Young Firm to anyone who needs a good attorney.

Conclusion

These eight individuals are just a few of the many offshore workers we have represented over the years, but their stories are illustrative of the overall experience of the injured maritime worker. Unlike onshore careers, the offshore life is fraught with difficulties even before an injury occurs. With the pressure to produce more faster, the often overlooked safety measures, and dangers of operating heavy and sometimes unreliable machinery, working offshore is no easy task.

Even harder is making the decision to do something about an offshore injury. No one wants to file against their employer, as you have seen with these men, but often this course of action is the only smart option to those injured in the maritime industry.

Many choose to ignore their situation or try to simply maintain the status quo, however, we can assure you that having a long-term plan that takes into account your injury, future ability to work, and medical expenses is by far the better decision.

If you have any questions at all or would like to discuss your situation, rights, and options, feel free to contact us anytime.

REAL PEOPLE
REAL RESULTS

Some required legal junk: Look, you're smart and you know your case is different from all other cases. Just because we list these past cases does not mean that you will get the exact same results. Heck, you may get more than our past clients did! The point is to select a good attorney who you can trust and who has gotten some serious results in the past.

$7,150,000

Fast Facts:
- Offshore incident
- Delayed treatment
- Paralysis & brain injury

Our client was delayed treatment for a "cavernous malformation" of a blood vessel on his brain stem, which resulted in complete paralysis. Earlier treatment could have greatly improved his final condition. He received a settlement that would provide money for him and his family for the rest of his life.

$3,500,000

Fast Facts:
- Offshore incident
- Stroke & brain injury
- Jones Act seaman

One of our clients, an injured Jones Act seaman, was unfortunate to have suffered a stroke while working offshore. He wasn't given the medical treatment he needed immediately and it cost him. Fortunately, we were able to get him the money he needed.

$2,560,000

Fast Facts:
- Crane collapse
- Vessel repair Supervisor
- Ankle & heel injury

A client a few years ago suffered a terrible experience when the crane he was operating collapsed due to a faulty weld and crashed into another building, killing our client's cousin who was also working at that time. Our client sustained debilitating injuries to his feet and had to get surgery several times. He was eventually awarded $2,560,000 from a New Orleans jury.

$2,400,000

Fast Facts:
- Barge incident
- Foot injury
- Permanent nerve damage

Our client was injured while moving a large tank of oxygen across the unsafe deck of a barge. The tank smashed into his ankle, severely injuring it. He now has permanent nerve damage and will walk with a limp for the rest of his life. The company fought hard but ultimately a jury awarded him a large amount that he could not get from the company on his own.

$1,900,000

Fast Facts:
- Offshore worker
- Derrick incident
- Leg injury

An offshore rig worker sustained severe nerve injury to his left leg resulting in significant disability as well as constant pain. He was hurt while working in the derrick aboard an offshore rig. The company claimed he was to blame for his accident, but we were able to prove that the company was actually at fault. As a result, he achieved a $1,900,000 settlement.

$1,400,000

Fast Facts:
- Jones Act case
- Judge verdict
- Lower back injury

Our client sustained an injury to his lower back, which, although it did not require surgery, prevented him from returning to offshore work where he was earning more than $40,000 per year. Prior to the trial, our client had settled with one of the defendants for $250,000. The verdict was settled during the appeal process.

$1,200,000

Fast Facts:
- Tug boat incident
- Hip injury
- Deckhand

A deckhand suffered a hip injury when he fell from his top bunk on a Golding Barge Line tug boat. Most other bunks on the tugs had been fixed but his bunk had not been modified yet simply because the company had not gotten around to it. Our client was extremely happy with the case results he received.

Why We Practice Maritime Law

My name is Timothy Young and for more than 20 years it has been my privilege to help injured offshore and maritime workers. Something deep inside of me is stirred whenever I know that a company is trying to take advantage of an honest, hard-working employee who has had a serious injury through no fault of his own.

Most often there is an employer/employee relationship, and to me that makes it all the worse when an employer is twisting the laws or facts to get out of paying what it should for the serious damages it caused to one of its own employees.

Most offshore and maritime workers would prefer not to file a suit. They would rather go on with their careers and turn back the clock to before the accident happened. I understand that. But hoping to change the past won't make the future any better.

What we do is not simply gather evidence

and experts to prove our client's claim in court. That's just the 'legal' part of it.

We also counsel our clients on their options and how to map out the best future they can have with the cards they were dealt. I can't think of a more important service we offer.

I often tell juries in closing arguments that they have a rare opportunity to help a fellow citizen and directly impact a person's life for the better. I tell them they should not waste that chance. I also feel we have that same opportunity with each new client we team up with.

I hope you found this book both helpful and encouraging during your current difficulties. Please phone us if you need anything or have any concerns you want to talk about.

Sincerely,
Tim Young

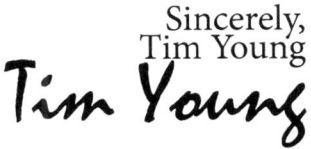

www.JonesActLaw.com

www.ingramcontent.com/pod-product-compliance
Lightning Source LLC
Chambersburg PA
CBHW041210180526
45172CB00006B/1230